STOP, DROP, and ROLL!

By CHARLES GHIGNA

Illustrations by GLENN THOMAS

Music by DREW TEMPERANTE

CANTATA
LEARNING

WWW.CANTATALEARNING.COM

CANTATA
LEARNING

Published by Cantata Learning
1710 Roe Crest Drive
North Mankato, MN 56003
www.cantatalearning.com

Library of Congress Cataloging-in-Publication Data
Names: Ghigna, Charles, author. | Thomas, Glenn, illustrator. | Temperante,
    Drew, composer.
Title: Stop, drop, and roll! / by Charles Ghigna ; illustrations by Glenn
    Thomas ; music by Drew Temperante.
Description: North Mankato, MN : Cantata Learning, [2018] | Series: Fire
    safety | Includes lyrics and sheet music. | Audience: Ages 3-8. |
    Audience: K to grade 3. | Includes bibliographical references.
Identifiers: LCCN 2017007517 (print) | LCCN 2017040838 (ebook) | ISBN
    9781684100521 | ISBN 9781684100514 (hardcover : alk. paper) | ISBN
    9781684100941 (pbk. : alk. paper)
Subjects: LCSH: Fire prevention--Juvenile literature. | Children's songs,
    English.
Classification: LCC TH9148 (ebook) | LCC TH9148 .G4527 2018 (print) | DDC
    613.6--dc23
LC record available at https://lccn.loc.gov/2017007517

978-1-68410-379-9 (hardcover)

Book design, Tim Palin Creative
Editorial direction, Flat Sole Studio
Executive musical production and direction, Elizabeth Draper
Music arranged and produced by Drew Temperante

ACCESS THE MUSIC!

SCAN CODE WITH MOBILE APP

CANTATALEARNING.COM

Printed in the United States   4698

TIPS TO SUPPORT LITERACY AT HOME

WHY READING AND SINGING WITH YOUR CHILD IS SO IMPORTANT

Daily reading with your child leads to increased academic achievement. Music and songs, specifically rhyming songs, are a fun and easy way to build early literacy and language development. Music skills correlate significantly with both phonological awareness and reading development. Singing helps build vocabulary and speech development. And reading and appreciating music together is a wonderful way to strengthen your relationship.

READ AND SING EVERY DAY!

TIPS FOR USING CANTATA LEARNING BOOKS AND SONGS DURING YOUR DAILY STORY TIME

1. As you sing and read, point out the different words on the page that rhyme. Suggest other words that rhyme.

2. Memorize simple rhymes such as Itsy Bitsy Spider and sing them together. This encourages comprehension skills and early literacy skills.

3. Use the questions in the back of each book to guide your singing and storytelling.

4. Read the included sheet music with your child while you listen to the song. How do the music notes correlate to the words of the song?

5. Sing along on the go and at home. Access music by scanning the QR code on each Cantata book. You can also stream or download the music for free to your computer, smartphone, or mobile device.

Devoting time to daily reading shows that you are available for your child. Together, you are building language, literacy, and listening skills.

Have fun reading and singing!

Fire **safety** starts with you! If you see flames get close, what should you do? Stop, drop, and roll! Learning these three steps will help keep you safe.

Now turn the page to **practice** this important fire safety skill. Remember to sing along!

Fire safety starts with you!
It's time to practice what to do.

If flames spread quickly all about,
stop, drop, and roll to put them out.

Stop! Don't run around.
Drop! Get on the ground.
Roll! Roll yourself about.

You can put the fire out!

Flames burn orange and red and blue.

Don't let them get close to you.

Keep your **distance** and stay safe.

But practice these moves, just in case!

Stop! Don't run around.

Drop! Get on the ground.

Roll! Roll yourself about.

You can put the fire out!

Fire safety starts with you!
It's time to practice what to do.

If flames spread quickly all about,
stop, drop, and roll to put them out.

Stop! Don't run around.
Drop! Get on the ground.
Roll! Roll yourself about.

You can put the fire out!

Now you know all the moves.
Show your friends these safety **grooves**.

What do you do? Stop, drop, and roll.
Put the flames out. That's your **goal**!

Stop! Don't run around.

Drop! Get on the ground.

Roll! Roll yourself about.

You can put the fire out!

SONG LYRICS
Stop, Drop, and Roll!

Fire safety starts with you!
It's time to practice what to do.
If flames spread quickly all about,
stop, drop, and roll to put them out.

Stop! Don't run around.
Drop! Get on the ground.
Roll! Roll yourself about.
You can put the fire out!

Flames burn orange and red and blue.
Don't let them get close to you.
Keep your distance and stay safe.
But practice these moves, just in case!

Stop! Don't run around.
Drop! Get on the ground.
Roll! Roll yourself about.
You can put the fire out!

Fire safety starts with you!
It's time to practice what to do.
If flames spread quickly all about,
stop, drop, and roll to put them out.

Stop! Don't run around.
Drop! Get on the ground.
Roll! Roll yourself about.
You can put the fire out!

Now you know all the moves.
Show your friends these safety grooves.
What do you do? Stop, drop, and roll.
Put the flames out. That's your goal!

Stop! Don't run around.
Drop! Get on the ground.
Roll! Roll yourself about.
You can put the fire out!

Stop, Drop, and Roll!

Hip Hop
Drew Temperante

Verse

1. Fire safe - ty starts with you! It's time to prac - tice what to do. If flames spread quick - ly all a - bout, stop, drop, and roll to put them out.

Chorus

Stop! Don't run a-round. Drop! Get on the ground. Roll! Roll your-self a - bout. You can put the fire out!

Verse 2
Flames burn orange and red and blue.
Don't let them get close to you.
Keep your distance and stay safe.
But practice these moves, just in case!

Chorus

Verse 3
Fire safety starts with you!
It's time to practice what to do.
If flames spread quickly all about,
stop, drop, and roll to put them out.

Chorus

Verse 4
Now you know all the moves.
Show your friends these safety grooves.
What do you do? Stop, drop, and roll.
Put the flames out. That's your goal!

Chorus

23

GLOSSARY

distance—the length between two things

goal—something that you work for

grooves—fun moves

practice—to do something over and over so you can get good at it

safety—the act of being safe

GUIDED READING ACTIVITIES

1. Draw your own poster showing stop, drop, and roll. Hang this poster in your home. It will help teach your family about fire safety.

2. Listen to the song again. Every time you hear the word stop, freeze in place. When you hear drop, get on the ground. When you hear roll, you know what to do! Can you keep up?

3. Why should you never run if your clothes catch on fire? Running fans the flames. It gives the flames more oxygen. What does rolling do? Ask an adult if you need help with the answer.

TO LEARN MORE

Bellisario, Gina. *Let's Meet a Firefighter*. Minneapolis: Millbrook Press, 2013.

Guard, Anara. *What If There Is a Fire?* North Mankato, MN: Capstone, 2012.

Murray, Laura. *The Gingerbread Man Loose on the Fire Truck*. New York: G.P. Putnam's Sons, 2013.

Tibbott, Julie. *Fire Dog Rescue (Curious George)*. Boston: Houghton Mifflin Harcourt, 2015.